Brick and Mortar Business for...
NEWBIES

**from the library of the
New Thrive Learning Institute**

Get Related Materials

from Our Free Library

Instant Access – Join Here

Click or type into your browser:

http://livesensical.com/go/byob/

LEGAL NOTICE:

Table of Contents

Introduction

So you've decided that you are interested in starting your own retail store, but you need a little bit of help in getting started; well you cam to the right place.

It is not easy to start a retail business, but it doesn't have to be too difficult either. All you really need is the right advice to help you figure out where to start. That is why this manual has been written.

This will be your comprehensive guide to starting your very own retail business. In this manual you will learn to:

1. Prepare your business plan
2. Where to start
3. Knowing your competition
4. Marketing
5. Insurance
6. Registrations, permits, and licensees
7. merchandising

Is It Right for Me?

For all of the many that have actually had the thought of starting their own business, most of them don't. There are a great many reasons why people don't take their ideals of running a business past thoughts alone. Perhaps they fear quitting the comforts of a regular paycheck. Some fear that they lack the intelligence or commitment to follow through with it.

It takes a lot of gumption for anyone to have the courage to start their own business. A retail business is one of the hardest businesses to run; even more so than a restaurant. The reason of course is the competition. There are literally millions of retail businesses currently in business across the world. Hundreds of thousands of these go under every year.

It can be a frustrating thing to do at times, but it can also be a very rewarding one as well. There are a great many reasons why a person might want to start their own retail business, but before you do, you should ask yourself these questions first.

1. Can I afford to open my own retail business?
2. Am I eligible for a loan from a bank?
3. Do I have the right attitude to start my own business?
4. What type of retail business do I want to own?
5. What type of retail business can I succeed in?
6. Can I handle the decision making process as a business owner?
7. How good am I at multi tasking?

8. Can I handle the stress of being a business owner?

9. Do I feel comfortable being someone else's boss?

10. How are my abilities in dealing with people?

11. Am I a self starter?

12. How well can I get organized?

13. Am I a driven enough person?

14. How will starting my own business affect my family?

If you can honestly answer yes to these questions, then you are a perfect candidate to own your own retail business. These are some of the most important questions that you can ask yourself when considering opening up your own business.

Anyone that can answer yes to these questions need not concern themselves with fears of not being a good business owner. You should just be sure to be really honest with yourself when giving your answers.

Why Should I Start My Own Business?

If you have already answered yes to the above, you should also consider why it would be a good idea to start your own retail business. There are many reasons to do this if you are a great initiator in life. Here are just some of the reasons to do so.

1. You can be your own boss. You won't have to answer to someone else's demands or criticisms.

2. You can set your own hours. You will no longer have to abide by any specifically set amount of hours, and your lunches are your own.

3. Your earning potential can be much higher when you own your own business.

4. It is a very exciting and unpredictable way of life. A great thing for those that like to experience changes in each and every day.

5. It is a chance to always learn new things and meet new and interesting people.

6. It is a good opportunity to do some good in your community by producing jobs, and helping with charities etc.

As you can see, there are a great many reasons why owning your own business can be a very rewarding experience in a great many ways. Of course there are many more, but we can only mention so many.

The Business Plan

Preparing your business plan is the most important part of getting started on your retail business. It is the best way for you to build your strategy and plan your course of action. A good business plan should include the following information.

1. What business you are planning to be in
2. Where your potential market is
3. Who your potential customers are
4. Who your competition is
5. Your sales strategy
6. What your merchandising method is going to be
7. How much money is needed to get started
8. How you will get the work done efficiently
9. What management controls are needed
10. When you should revise your business plan, and how often
11. Where you can go for help

These are just some of the things that you are going to have to include in your business plan. A properly written business plan will cover all of the basic requirements for starting and maintaining a successful business. A business plan is nothing more than a plan of action for you to follow. It is like your instruction manual that you will write for yourself.

You will need your business plan when you go to a bank or investor for money to help you start your business. It will provide its reader with all of the information about your business and how you plan to succeed at it. Not to mention, it will provide you with the help that you need when dealing with a hard situation.

The business plan also makes for a handy reference for your potential employees and managers. When you devise your business plan you should bear in mind that knowing your market is the best chance that you have at being successful in your field.

A successful business plan will cover every aspect of your retail business and have a plan of action in accordance to it. It is an essential aspect of starting a retail business.

What Kind of Business Do I Want?

There are just so many things to consider when wanting to start your own business. You would think that the questions set above would be enough, but of course, like all things in life, beginning your own business is more complicated than that. There are three basic types of business' that you will have to choose from when you are considering the start of your own business. They are as follows:

Sole Proprietorship

A sole proprietorship is a business that has only one owner. There can be many benefits and pitfalls to running your business as a sole proprietor.

The Benefits:

- You can keep more of your businesses money's earned.
- There are less hassles than there might be with other proprietors.
- You can run the business in any manner that you please.
- It is the least costly way of starting a business.
- It is easier to get your business started and apply for your permits, licensees etc.
- Dealing with the issue of taxes is less complicated and cheaper.

Pitfalls:

- It is more costly when the business is faced with

losses

- All responsibility falls solely upon the proprietors shoulders

- All of the costs that go along with maintaining the business keeping it running smoothly are solely the owner's.

- All decisions are made at the owner's discretion

- Basically, everything is the owner's responsibility.

There are many reasons why you should consider running a business on your own. However, you do have other options.

Partnership

There are many types of partnerships that you can delve into. The most commonly chosen are general partnerships and limited partnerships. General partnerships can be entered into with a mere oral agreement or you can have lawyers draw up legal and binding partnership documents.

If you are considering the idea of having a partnership you should know that signing a legal partnership agreement is the best way to go about it. The legal fees for these documents are more costly than a sole proprietorship, but not as expensive as in a corporation.

When you decide to enter into a partnership, you should be certain to add only the specifics of the agreement that you can both agree to. Here is a list of some of the other things that you should have placed in a partnership agreement.

- The type of business that you plan to run

- The correct amount of equity that both parties will invest

- How you will divide your profits and losses
- How much you will each be compensated
- How you will divide your profits and losses
- How long will plan to be in business together
- Set up provisions for any changes made and closing down
- Dispute settlement clause
- Restriction of authority and expenditures
- **A reasonable settlement in case one partner dies or is incapacitated**

As you can see, there are a great many things to consider when starting a partnership. As with running a sole proprietorship, there are a lot of benefits and pitfalls as well. I have listed them here for you.

Benefits

- The cost of investing in the business is cheaper since they are divided among two people instead of one.
- The money needed to process legal fees and everything else that requires money is cheaper.
- There is assistance in dealing with the everyday tasks like, merchandising, employee issues, general dealings with the public, and all general business concerns.
- With two people running the business, each can have more time with their families and friends
- Legal matters are cheaper for both

- A partnership generally makes the profits and revenue much higher.

- Losses are shared by both and are thus actually easier to deal with

Pitfalls

1. Complications may arise if both parties are not in agreement about decisions

2. Profits must be divided among the two and are therefore lower for each

3. One partner may wish to be let out of the business if things are not running smoothly (this can be a problem if you are only using an oral agreement)

4. Partners may not agree on when to end the business

5. Compensation problems can occur if one partner puts up more equity in the business and the other wants to be compensated in the same manner

Corporation

Corporation can make the start of a new business very much easier, but it also takes a great deal more money and much more paperwork in order to make it happen. Generally, it is best when beginning a retail business to avoid starting up as a corporation.

Usually corporations do not run with any specific person claiming themselves as the owner. In a corporation, control generally depends on whoever owns the most stock. It is most common that you must own at least 51% of the stock in the corporation in order to have control of the company.

There are also many more rules that you must follow in order to run any business as a corporation as well. In a corporation you must hold regular meetings of the board of directors which generally consists of 10 people. All of whom are to make decisions regarding the business.

You must also host stockholder's meetings as well and keep viable records of all the decisions that are made. There can be any number of stockholders present for these meetings.

Corporations are best left for extremely large retail business ideas because of the complications that can arise in running a corporation. Some of these problems can be as follows:

- Constant battling over stocks

- Backbiting is always a problem when so many people are involved in a business deal.

- People are often trying to buy out other stockholders so as to gain control over the businesses decisions; especially if it is successful

- As corporations are generally formed with the intent on becoming a chain of retail outlets or franchises, it can be a very costly venture to take for the average business owner.

What Type of Business Should I Start?

If you are reading this, then you already have an idea of what sort of business you should start, but it is always good to consider this idea thoroughly. There are many retail businesses on the market today, and most of them are already in place. It is best that you consider what type of business that you feel you would have the most success in.

One of the ways that you can accomplish this is to know exactly what is lacking in the market around you. However before you even consider starting your own retail business there are a few questions that you should ask yourself first.

Where Is My Expertise?

It is best that you open a business that isn't too complicated for you to understand the ins and outs of. You need to know everything there is to any aspect of the business before you consider running one of your own. Otherwise, you are setting yourself up for failure.

You don't necessarily need to be an "expert" in the business, but a basic understanding is a good place to start. A desire for your expected merchandise is a good thing also. You wouldn't want to open a car dealership if you didn't already have a certain amount of interest in cars because you will find that learning about them may not interest you. You can't expect to sell any cars if you don't have some knowledge on them first.

As with starting any business, you will need to be able to explain your business to your future employees as well. You cannot expect your employees to know everything on their own, and you can't direct them without some knowledge beforehand either.

What Type of Business Am I interested In?

Whenever you think about starting a business, you should know what type of business that you want to open. There a few different ways that you can go about figuring this out because there are so many types of retail businesses out there to choose from. Some of them are:

- **Retail Franchises**: Franchises are businesses that you can buy into that are already on the market. They are generally already popular. You may want to buy into a Gap retail outlet or Nike store. The good thing about buying into a franchise retail business is that you already know that it is a popular idea. It can cut some of your work in half. Of course, you will still need to ensure that you are buying into a viable choice for your locale.

- **Online Retailing**: These are more centered around selling your products on the Internet. It is a cheaper method of beginning your retail outlet as there is not a necessary need for leasing a new property, you can simply display pictures of your products and post them online for people to purchase by credit card. However cheaper it may be, online retail chains do not have a better record of success than the standard retail outlet, it is just a cheaper way of having one.

- **General Merchant Store**: When most people think of opening a retail business this is what they are talking about. This is an actual store set up on a leased piece of property. You will have to go through a great deal of research and finances in order to open one of these, but the benefits can be outstanding. This is the type of business that this manual generally talks about.

Knowing which of these types of retail businesses you would feel more comfortable in conducting is the best way to begin. You may not want to buy into a franchise, but then again, you might. In order to know which of these best suits you, you have to know yourself and your abilities pretty well first.

If you do choose to buy into a franchise, you should be fully aware of what that company is about, and how you can best add your own personal touch to it.

Starting a retail business from an established idea as in a clothing outlet, is a sure fire way to start because as there are already clothing outlets on the market, you can be sure to add what you think would make a good addition to the market or you can change what you think needs to be changed as a consumer.

It gets pretty tricky though when you are trying to open a retail outlet that hasn't already been on the market before. If you plan to begin your very own retail concept, you must spend an extra amount of time on your business plan if you are to convince the loan officer, and your potential customers that you are providing a service that they will indeed need.

It is very difficult to offer a product that hasn't been on the market yet or if you are planning on beginning a business that is selling something that is not generally available. For this type of venture you will need to thoroughly assess your potential market first. This type of work flows directly into the next section.

Know Your Market

Before you decide to start any retail business, you must know what the market is for your specific type of business. You do not want to open a retail outlet for clothing if your locale has nine different malls that are filled with clothing outlets.

Generally when a person decides to open a retail business it is because they have observed a need for a certain type of product in their neighborhood. To get the precise amount of knowledge to be successful, you will need to do your research. Part of this research is knowing what the market is like.

You will obviously want to know what the consumer demand is. That just means you will want to know what the consumers need so that you can provide it to them. You certainly don't want to open a store in an area that already has 12 just like it because then you are lessening your chances of success.

Quick Tip: 80% of new retail businesses fail within their first year of business.

You certainly do not want to be a statistic. Naturally, choosing the right market to start your business is just the first step in choosing the right retail outlet to invest your time and money in. You will also want to know what your competition is.

In order for you to properly assess your potential market you will have to do your research. Here are some of the popular ways that companies use in order to do this.

Surveys

Companies will often use market surveys when they want to test the market with their customers. You can conduct question and answer periods with consumers, written surveys that ask your consumers what they want and how they would like to receive it, you can conduct hidden surveys, which is where your consumers do not know that they are being monitored.

Surveys are a very popular method that companies use to get consumer opinions. They are also used in order to get a consumer's opinion about their competition's products and services also. When you conduct a survey it is good to offer some sort of incentive or gift from the people that are volunteering their time, you can get a better response that way.

Product Testing

Everyone has heard of product testing. This is just when one company places their product against another's so that they try to convince consumers that theirs is better. Of course it would serve you best advertise the results if they are positive.

Product testing is also a way for a new company to learn what is wrong with their merchandise before it reaches the market. It is a good way to get the general opinion of your potential consumers before you officially open for business. It helps get the "kinks" out first.

Offering a Pre-Opening

This is a lot like hosting a sneak preview to a movie. This is where you can invite a select number of people into your retail outlet so that they can catch a glimpse of what you are hoping to accomplish.

You must understand that this is not the same as actually letting people into your leased property. This is more of allowing them to see what your idea is and offering a look at it in its expected reality. To do this, you would have to project a video replication of your stores concept. This gives potential consumers a chance to see your idea before them, without you having to spend all of the money that it takes to begin a business first.

This is becoming a popular way for people to get an idea of your business and for you to get their reaction to your idea without having to make it a full realization first. You can also make a computer generated CD Rom if you find it cheaper or easier.

Know Your Strengths

You need to know what you can do and what you can't do if you are going to run your own retail business. It isn't going to serve you well if you try to manage your own accounts if you are not very good at book keeping. Here is a list of some of the things that you are going to have to know about if you want to run your own retail business.

- **Basic Book keeping:** So that you can keep an accurate account of all of the money you owe, the money owed to you, and what is left afterwards.

- **Stock and inventory:** You have to be able to keep track of how much merchandise you have; how much you need to order, and how to arrange it properly.

- **Merchandising:** You want to be able to arrange your merchandise in an appealing way.

- **Payroll:** You have to be able to keep enough money to pay employees and keep track of monies paid.

- **Marketing:** You will need to know how to market your store, keep up with demand, and monitor the buying trends of your customers.

- **Basic economics:** You will need to be able to follow the economic trends so that you can maintain a profit for your business.

- **Networking:** It is necessary for you to gather and maintain business contacts. They will prove invaluable to you at times.

These are just some of the things that you are going to have to know in order to maintain a good business. If you find that you will have problems doing some of these things, then you should get someone else to handle them for you. Better that than lose money in the end.

Know Your Competition

Once you have decided what type of retail business is best for you, you need to know who your competition is. Knowing this will help you to decide what your plan of action will be in dealing with them.

You will want to know what their successes have been and what their pitfalls have been as well. You will want to avoid making the same mistakes that they have, but it is always good to know what works as well if you plan to compete. In some cases, you may find that the best way to compete with your competition is to not compete at all, especially if they have established a long and trusted reputation with their consumers. In this case, you will want to compete with them without competing with them at all. Below are some ways that you can do that.

You do not want to alienate your competition or build feuds with them because they can be a source of great help to you if you know how to approach them. Here are some good examples of ways that you can create a good rapport with them.

- **Offer to be an affiliate of theirs.** This way you can ensure that they will send business your way if they cannot meet the present needs of a customer that you can supply.

- **Offer to not place certain items on your shelves that they stock and ask them to do the same.** Grocery stores have this idea down pat. What they do is divide certain popular goods among themselves so that only each chain only serves certain hard to find items that are popular. This ensures that each chain will not be in direct competition for certain items. Each gets their own special item that none other contains. It is a great way to promote one another without causing any problems. This is a nice way to cross advertise.

- **Do not place your store directly across from any major competition.** Doing this will only give you a 50% chance of success; lower if they are already long since established. Satisfied customers rarely wander into the new competitor's store.

- **Try to market your prices at a better bargain than your competitors.** If you can't, place your inventory in a more satisfactory arrangement. Sometimes it is all about the appearance of things.

- **Assess your competitor's success rate.** Learn what they are doing that is so great and offer something better or at a more reasonable price.

These are just some of the things that you can do to present yourself in the best light possible when dealing with your competition. Of course nothing beats putting yourself in your consumers' position. You must think of of what you would like in a retail outlet so that you can best compete in the market.

You should also keep your eye on their marketing and promotional techniques because it will help you to keep up with them better. All of this stuff should be placed directly in your business plan if you want to show that you are prepared for the tasks and potential problems that can arise.

You will want to know how the competition is faring in the market also. You do not want to get into a market that is already unsuccessful. You must assume that if your competition is doing badly, that the market isn't as good as you may have hoped. Naturally you should double check your information because it is possible that your competition may just not be meeting the current demand properly. If this is the case, then you should look for the best way to meet the need in a better manner.

Registrations Permits and Licensing

After you have met the above mentioned requirements for starting your business, and you've decided to follow through, you will need to apply for all of the needed permits and licenses that you may require. Some of these can include:

Business Registration

You will have to register the name of your retail business before you can place it on the market. You will need to think of a name that is catchy and easy to remember. The law requires you to register your business' name so that no other company uses the same name as you do.

Each State and Municipality have their own laws regarding this so you would be better off asking your local registrars office what the proper procedure is beforehand. Registering your business will ensure that your retail business has its own business number that you can use when setting up accounts with warehouses that host your merchandise.

Vendors Permits

You will also need to register for your vendors permits. This is basically a piece of paper that states that you are legally allowed to charge money for certain merchandise. Your vendors permit should be placed in an area that is visible to the public at all times.

The reason that you need a vendor's permit is because you will also have to charge taxes on your merchandise. You can't tax your merchandise without a vendor's permit. Permits are always very particular, so you will need to include the exact type of merchandise that you plan to sell in order to receive the correct permit.

If you are planning to open a clothing outlet, but want to add some food items to your shelves, you will need a special permit to sell both. That is why you want to make sure that you are very specific with the type of permit that you request.

Taxes

Believe it or not, you also have to register for a special tax number so that you can charge the taxes to your customers. You need this number because each time you process a purchase and charge the necessary taxes, the taxes go directly to the internal revenue service. If you don't charge taxes to your customers, then you will be responsible to pay all of that money yourself.

You must file the yearly taxes with the IRA each fiscal year end. This means that your business taxes are due every year around the same time as you first began your business. You would have a lot to account for if you didn't charge any taxes to your customers and if you weren't properly registered with your local tax service.

Insurance

Although it is not necessary that you apply for insurance on your residential property, you must apply for insurance on your business property. With the crime rate being what it is, you have to have insurance. But there are at least 3 types that you must apply for when starting your own retail business, and they are:

1. **Workman's compensation:** You have to be able to support your employees should they get hurt on the job. You as the employers have to apply for this from a private insurance company.

2. **Liability Insurance:** This is in the event that a consumer is injured on your property. At the least you have to apply for 'limited liability" insurance.

3. **Property:** Naturally this type of insurance will protect you in the event of a fire or theft etc. It just helps to know that you can regain some of your property or merchandise back in case of a disaster or crisis.

Choosing the Right Location

As with the purchase or lease of any property, you will have to take into account the location that it is in. You cannot expect to run a successful retail business if you lease a property that is in a district that doesn't support the type of environment that would suit your business.

A good example: An expensive clothing store would not do very well in an impoverished neighborhood. You must consider that your business should be appropriate for the area that it is placed in.

Secondly, you do not want to place a discount retail outlet right next door to another one that sells the same products that you do. It just doesn't make sense. You want to choose an area that will set your store up as a unique place of business. You will want to stand out. You cannot stand out in an area that is filled with retail businesses that are along the exact same lines as yours.

If you do choose to set up in an area like this, then you have to be sure that you can bring something to the table so that you can compete with others. A great marketing and advertising campaign is a good place to start.

Marketing

This is something that you will already have an idea about when you plan your business plan. Nothing is better for an emerging retail business than a really good marketing strategy. This is when all of your research will work to your advantage. In order to build a good marketing strategy you must first:

- Correctly assess your competition and what they are doing to market their businesses. You have to offer your consumers something that is fresh and different if you want to get their attention.

- Survey your potential market beforehand so that you can establish what your consumers are missing in their current needs as consumers. You will want to know what they want and give it to them.

- Learn what types of advertisements work best in your business' locale. Sometimes commercials are best whereas other area get a better response by utilizing the local newspaper or pennysaver.

- Begin your promotion before you plan to open so that you can garner an interest in your merchandise before you open. Building up some interest ahead of time can help to ensure a good grand opening.

- Promotions and discounts are a necessity to running a successful retail business. You must make sure that you are in a position to compete in this manner. Your "grand opening" will run a lot better if you begin with a special promotion.

- The key to successful marketing will be your ability to

meet the basic supply and demand of your community. Be sure to stay on top of this because these things are always changing.

- You should be able to keep up with market changes and try to anticipate them beforehand because it keeps you a step ahead of the average consumer. This will prove invaluable to you later.

Merchandising and Inventory

Since the sole purpose of opening a retail business is to sell merchandise to the public, you should be certain to know exactly what types of merchandise you plan to sell, and also to know which merchandise to include in your store. You don't want to try and offer clothing and dog food in the same establishment if you are not planning on opening a department store.

This may sound silly, but many stores that fail offer merchandise that doesn't seem to make sense when mixed together. You would be surprised at how many retailers make this mistake.

When thinking about your merchandise you should also consider the correct positioning of it. This can often be the difference between selling your goods and not selling them. For example, you should place your sales items in an obvious and easy to spot place if you want that promotion to be seen. As a courtesy to your customers, you should consider placing private items in a less conspicuous area of your store. It just shows that you care about your customer's feelings.

When stocking your inventory, you should place like items together. If you were to open a car dealership, you would want to place your convertibles together and your vans together because it is a bit more slightly, but also because any consumer that is looking to buy a convertible would not want to have to travel all over the place just to find the one they like the best.

You will also want to place accessory items together and in a nearby position because they will be more likely to be purchased if they are near the item that it best fits with an din plain view.

Common Mistakes for New Businesses

As mentioned a bit earlier, at least 80% of new businesses fail within their first year of being open. There are many reasons why businesses tend to fail, and it is best to list them here so that you can try to avoid making these common mistakes when you open your retail business.

Advertising

Many new businesses fail to advertise properly. It wouldn't occur to most business owners that insufficient advertising might cause a problem with keeping their business afloat, but during tough times, advertising might be your best weapon.

When the economy is running badly, you should have enough money put aside to advertise special promotions and sales to your customers. When you do advertise, you should try to be everywhere. You want people to see your businesses name no matter where they turn. Here are some of the ways that you can advertise to ensure that you cannot be forgotten.

- Newspaper and magazine ads
- Newspaper, and direct mailbox inserts
- Flyers and posts
- Commercial and media ads
- Websites, complete with online store

You should know that these do not have to cost you an arm and a leg. Commercials can be costly, but these others don't have to be. Running a website can be free or cheap, and the software to host your own online store can also be cheap or free. You just need someone that can keep track of orders for you.

Improper advertising can leave the community not knowing that your business exists; especially during hard times. You want to stay available to all of your customers because if you disappear from view, so will your customers.

Improper book-keeping

It doesn't matter what you do to keep your business running at its best. If you do not keep proper track of your money's coming and goings, you will eventually be left with none.

If it is at all possible, do your own book keeping so that you know exactly where your money is going. If you do not know much about it, you should hire someone that does, but also someone that you can trust. If you must, hire someone just to watch the book keeper so that you don't get ripped off.

As the business owner, you need to know exactly how much money that your business has. You should know exactly how much profit that you are gaining each month so that you can use your money wisely. It is not always easy to keep track of all of your money, especially if you are generating a lot of business, but it doesn't have to be impossible.

Even with a good book keeper, you should look into popular accounting software like Quark Express and Microsoft Money because they do most of the work for you. All you really have to do yourself is add the right numbers and let the software add and subtract for you.

Every year many businesses go under due to bad book keeping. They spend money they don't have or they make errors processing payroll deposits. Don't let that happen to you.

Credit Problems

The worst thing that a business owner can do is to run it on too much credit. Each day it gets easier and easier for new businesses to gain credit accounts and credit cards from various companies. All too often, these companies run up more credit than they can repay.

It just goes to say that you have to live and run your business within your means. All too often business owners find themselves buying things that the business simply doesn't need. They also buy things for themselves on company credit. This is a big no-no in the business world.

Once a business spends too much money on credit, they learn all too late that the interest rates on credit cards can force hundreds of extra dollars in expenses. New and small retail businesses just can't afford to pay them. There is also the fact that over buying supplies and merchandise can be a far bigger problem than businesses expect.

Over paying employees can run any business into the ground if they are not keeping up with their regular expenses properly. Any successfully run business owner knows that you start off small, and hopefully build your way up. That is impossible if you are living and running your business above your means.

Opening at the Wrong Time

It is impossible to succeed at business if you open your business in a bare market. You do not want to choose the wrong time to host a grand opening. If you are trying to open your retail business during a depression for example, you will undoubtedly fail unless it is a dollar store that you are planning on.

Even a dollar store can fail under a depression because they rarely sell anything that is essentially needed. Some things they do sell are needed but most are simply knick knacks that are of little importance.

As a budding entrepreneur, you will have to keep up with economic trends. These days, the economy is constantly changing. You should avoid opening your retail business during an economic collapse. If at all possible you want to open your business during a steady economic period or when your market is on the rise. That is not always possible, but you must try.

Unreasonable Prices

It is really common sense, but many companies have a tendency to over charge their customers. It sounds like an easy thing to avoid, but sometimes, a business owner might have to charge more money for their wares because of financial difficulties or tax problems.

Many business owners take advantage of adverse economic situations and over charge as a means of capitalizing off of the consumers desperate needs. This can be devastating to any business if others aren't doing this or if the demand just doesn't meet the standard that the owner might have predicted.

Tax Problems

You would be surprised at how often a business owner fails to properly deal with the taxes on their goods and property. It would seem to be an easily dealt with issue, but the unseasoned proprietor can easily fall prey to the IRS.

Poor calculation can be a costly problem, but failing to properly fill out your tax forms, and missing valuable monies can be a problem as well. Sometimes it is simply an issue of filing your taxes late. Keeping up with your fiscal year's end can be frightfully easy to forget. A good accountant is a need to avoid common tax problems like these and others.

Poor Location

It is very easy to fall into the common problem of choosing a poor location for your retail business, but it happens every day. Businesses that open in a hard to get to area often find themselves without customers, but this is not the only problem with location.

Sometimes a business can be greatly situated but be poorly accommodated. Basically, this is when a proprietor buys or leases a damaged piece of property. Sometimes a person can be in such in a hurry to garner the property that they fail to see its flaws. This can run up a lot of debt in trying to salvage it.

You should always try to ask why the business that was there before you went under. Whoever the Realtor is sure to know the details. If they don't I wouldn't trust that Realtor. A failure to keep any piece of real estate is a common problem of the inexperienced proprietor.

Before you agree to take on any property, you should have knowledge of the property's background. You should have someone with you that knows the basics of plumbing and all of the other property damage that the average person cannot see.

Summary

By now, you should know if owning a retail business of your own is right for you. If you have, you have learned all of the things that you will need to be aware of in order to get it up and running. Hopefully you have also realized that running your own business takes a lot more than mere desire.

What I have not mentioned yet is how you can get the start up money for your business, so I will write a little bit about it now. Since getting money is relatively self explanatory, I though it unnecessary to give it a full section. Here a the different ways that you can get the money to run your own business.

1. You can apply for a loan

2. You can borrow money from friends or separate loan companies.

3. You can take the money from your savings

That is about all that I feel is needed in knowing where you can get your start up money. Of course you can always check your government listings as there are some places in the government that will help you with your start up costs.

In this guide you have learned to:

- Decide if you have what it takes to start your own retail business

- How to chose the right business for you

- The benefits and pitfalls to owning your own retail business

- What must be done in order to start your own business.

- What types of licensees and permits that you will need while running your own business
- Whether or not to be a partnership, sole proprietor, or corporation
- Problems that can arise by owning your own business
- Marketing
- How to avoid common mistakes made by first time owners
- Merchandising and inventory
- Choosing the right location
- How to know your strengths
- The business plan
- Knowing your market

Bonus

Get Related Materials

from Our Free Library

Instant Access – Join Here

Click or type into your browser:

http://livesensical.com/go/byob/

www.ingramcontent.com/pod-product-compliance
Lightning Source LLC
Chambersburg PA
CBHW021941170526
45157CB00005B/2379